Do you know . . .

- how to make first-class finds at secondhand stores?

- when the smartest time to shop is?

- where the best buys can be found?

- how to avoid buying damaged goods (or figure out if they're worth fixing)?

- how to bargain down to the lowest possible price?

- how auctions work—and how to make them work for you?

Now you can find out—
and learn how to make the most
of thrift shops, garage sales, flea markets,
and more—
in . . .

SAVE YOURSELF A FORTUNE!

$AVE YOURSELF A FORTUNE!

THE
BARGAIN HUNTER'S GUIDE
TO

FLEA MARKETS • THRIFT SHOPS
YARD SALES • AUCTIONS
ANTIQUE STORES • ESTATE SALES
AND MORE!

JODY BAMEL

BERKLEY BOOKS, NEW YORK

SAVE YOURSELF A FORTUNE!

A Berkley Book / published by arrangement with
the author

PRINTING HISTORY
Berkley edition / August 1995

ISBN: 0-425-14882-3

BERKLEY®
Berkley Books are published by The Berkley Publishing Group,
200 Madison Avenue, New York, New York 10016.
BERKLEY and the "B" design
are trademarks belonging to Berkley Publishing Corporation.

PRINTED IN THE UNITED STATES OF AMERICA

10 9 8 7 6 5 4 3 2 1

Contents

Contents

Introduction

I have always been afraid to write this book, afraid that if more people knew these secrets there would be no bargains left for the truly devoted thrift shopper like myself. I have been afraid to tell, for fear I would create more smart shoppers who might snap up a bargain before I got to it. Thrift shoppers are turning up everywhere in record numbers, ordinary people like you and me shopping for quality at the lowest bargain prices possible. Some of them are seasoned shoppers, but many more are joining the ranks.

For those of you who already know the ins and outs of successful thrift shopping, this book will sharpen your skills. For those of you who are new to the joys of bargain hunting, fear not. The secrets are simple and only require imagination and a little know-how. There are multitudes of incredible buys in the category of "slightly used." For the hesitant and the squeamish, may I remind you that antiques are also in the category of "slightly used," but they are more than one hundred years old—(maybe they should be considered "very used")—and have a fancy label. Thrift shoppers concentrate mostly on rather new or collectible things, but even antiques pop up in many second-hand stores and sales. In fact, antiques dealers are thrift shoppers, too; they are just more seasoned and knowledgeable about what they are looking for and where to find it. The secret of gaining more knowledge is about to be revealed to you. I ask only one favor in return: Save some for me.

SAVE YOURSELF A FORTUNE!

The Increasing Ranks

To my knowledge there are no actual statistics about thrift shopping, so I made the rounds of all the proprietors and volunteers I am acquainted with and asked lots of questions. I got lots of answers.

Ann, who has worked at my local Salvation Army for years, was more than happy to tell me about the new breed of shoppers. Their regulars are made up of a variety of folks: two lawyers who come every Friday to see what the new arrivals are; a judge and his wife; tons of teens shopping for unique clothing; and a mixture of moms buying clothing for their kids. On "bag day" (you can fill up a large garbage bag supplied by the store with any clothing you want for a lump sum of $22) the place is swamped from 8 A.M. till closing, with businessmen and women, families, teenagers, grandmas, construction workers, and pretty much everyone and his or her brother. The event itself is promoted with a little advertising, in-store flyers, and people like me who just ask when the next "bag day" is happening. It draws the team of regular thrift hunters and anyone else who gets wind of it.

Ann says most of the patrons are usually nice, with a few exceptions. The Salvation Army pays its employees, but a lot of thrift-shop workers are volunteers, so please remember to treat them well. Don't forget your manners in the bargain frenzy. She remembers her regulars, and their dispositions as well. When it comes time for her to determine a price, nice begets nice.

At my town thrift shop, Mary (who has been the manager for many years) tells me that donations and profits have increased more than three times over the last five years. The location, in a walk-around town, brings in just about every type of person from browsers to regular buyers. I took my parents there, and they couldn't help trying on clothing and scouting the racks. Her customers are from all walks of life—secretaries, hairdressers, attorneys, students, mothers, fathers, kids, and pretty much anyone and everyone looking for a find. A lot of people bring their kids, but not all of them let the kids shop on their own. I encourage you to do this. Encourage the children to make their own deals and pick their own prizes. It's a lesson in value and humility, along with a chance for a great feeling of success when they find a bargain of their own.

My parents used to take me "antiquing," before it was popular. Most of the "antiques" stores were piles of furniture, housewares, and bric-a-brac in no particular semblance of order. I did my own digging and began a collection of antique purses by buying them (as my mother would tell the owner of the store) with my baby-sitting money. The owners happily sold me beautiful beaded bags for two and three dollars which are now worth a great deal more. It gave me a sense of pride learning about collecting (after all, I had to learn that these were not the usual toys) and turned me into the avid thrift shopper I am today. I was lucky it was for fun, but I learned how to stretch a dollar and the confidence to haggle a bargain when I had to spend my own money. I vividly remember the store and my first pocketbook purchase, especially since it was the same day my father drove halfway home and then returned to the store to buy a marble pedestal he couldn't get out of his mind. He said, "If you can't walk away from it—buy it. Life's too short to have little regrets." I will discuss little regrets again later.

In preparing this book, I asked a lot of store workers for their best stories. The best one came from Mary at my hometown thrift shop on Long Island. A young girl came in one day looking for a wedding dress. She browsed around, picked the one she wanted, and then ran out the back door without paying! Now, most thrift shops will give you anything you are in need of without much problem anyway, but I guess the girl figured it was easier just to run off with the dress. What a great way to start a marriage. Can you imagine her at the altar saying, "I do, and guess what, honey, I stole my dress. Won't I just be the perfect wife?"

There are two more things you should know when doing these secondhand shopping sprees. When shopping with a friend, choose a partner whose taste is different from your own. Unless you are willing to give up some of your finds, shopping with a friend with the same taste or size will create a few tense situations. Also, don't dress in your Sunday best. If you're fortunate enough to be thrift shopping for fun, remember that there are thousands of people doing it out of necessity, and it looks quite improper to be bargaining down the dollars when you're dressed in diamonds and fur.

Thrift-Shopping Personalities

There are various types of thrift-shopping personalities. The traits are inside all of us just waiting for an opportunity to surface. You may not know which type you are at the moment, but it is good to identify the different qualities so as to avoid the pitfalls that may follow. For instance, the bargain shopper will always buy excellent bargains but will often buy something unneccessary just because it *is* a bargain. This is a very good way to fill up a residence with future garage-sale material. A bargain is only a bargain if it has a proper use in the near future. Buying for the sake of getting a bargain will only leave a shopper with piles of purposeless purchases. The up side is that even if the jeans you bought for $1.50 don't fit when you get them home, you can always donate them back to a thrift shop and take a tax deduction. It's the beauty of the American way. Taking a chance on an item or two at the right price is rarely a total loss. But the small purchases do add up; "restraint" is an important word to keep in mind on the thrift-shopping circuit. In the beginning stages of shopping, it will be difficult to resist the call of the bargain. As you become more adept, you will be able to curb your buying powers and reserve them for what you really seek.

The next type, the fun shopper, merely enjoys the looking and finding. Not all fun shoppers even intend to buy, and many are content just to hunt and locate. The fun shopper is helpful to have around for those of us who lose control, because they remind us of the uselessness of some of our purchases. After all, how many of us actually have use for an eleven-foot bronze figurative sculpture of Hannibal and his elephants? Fun shoppers have an unbiased observer's view that makes them a pleasure to take along, without the threat of their beating you to the bargain you really want. They are content to get lucky once in a while and don't long for the joy of the purchase every time.

Many of us fit into my "obsessive collector" category. Most of us collect something: tools, cat paraphernalia, comic books, cars, pewter, software—the list is endless. Obsessive collectors are very active. They research, read, and physically look in order find their collectibles in the most likely places for the best price. They keep track mentally of where they have had their greatest success and retrace their steps to increase their collections. There are methods to accomplish this feat, which I will describe in detail later on. It is not as difficult as some people believe. Usually it just requires practice, and the novice needs only to keep shopping to become an expert. I am an obsessive collector of Russel Wright dinnerware. I began my collecting innocently enough, purchasing two serving pieces for two dollars at an obscure garage sale that I happened on while driving in upstate New York. I bought the pieces because I liked their design and color, not because I knew what they were or who designed them. It was a year or so later that my friend John Brencale saw them on my dining room buffet and told me he had two mugs with saucers to match them. When he brought them over and gave them to me on his next visit, I realized that there must be full sets of dinnerware to go along with my serving pieces. I began searching for scores of these dishes at garage sales, thrift shops, tag sales, and bazaars. (Not to mention asking all my friends and their relatives if they had any, and a few of them did!)

My next step was to take out books from the library about the era the dishes were from and other pieces and styles designed by Mr. Wright. I became familiar with many of the pieces, so as to recognize them in my shopping travels. I went further to discover that many antiques dealers were interested in acquiring depression glass and would be willing to trade depression glass for the Russel Wright I desired. I spent three months studying (not eight hours a day, just light reading) to learn markings and styles of depression glassware, and then went on to buy a lot of it cheap and trade it off. A considerable amount of my Wright collection was acquired by this method. Trading was fun and opened new doors for me, of sources and knowledge about my precious collection and other desired collectibles. I learned to keep my eyes open for items that could be traded or resold to fuel my collection.

Another avenue for the obsessive or extremely dedicated collector is what I refer to as show and tell. My friends and family all know what I collect, and have been shown and have used my collectibles, so they are likely to recognize it when they see it somewhere. They have unknowingly become fun shoppers assisting in increasing my collection. It is fun to shop for someone else's collectible. You get the joy of the find, the thrill of the bargain, and you don't even have to buy it yourself. My shoppers can either tell me about a bargain or snatch it up and get the money from me later or give the item as a gift in the future. Plenty of people have purchased Russel Wright gifts for me in unlikely places. I have pieces from Nebraska, Massachusetts, California, and everywhere my close kin and friends have traveled. It's nice to have them think of me when they see things that I collect, even if they don't buy them. They are on the lookout for my collection, and in return I search for the things that they are trying to find. It's a form of trading that expands your buying territory to anywhere your friends and family may be.

To make my own gift-giving easier, I carry

around a list of friends' and family members' clothing sizes and always keep in mind their decor and taste. You never know when the perfect gift will surface. It is rewarding to find the perfect something for a special person. I once found a beautiful dark-green glass vase for my friend Marcy at a garage sale. I thought of her the second I saw it, because her house is done in hunter-green, white, and pink. When I uncovered the vase from behind a bunch of junk, it was disgustingly dirty, but I saw the potential, paid the five dollars, and put it through the dishwasher a few times, until it sparkled. It turned out to be such beautiful blown glass that I almost didn't give it to Marcy. I packed it away for the next Christmas (it even moved with me once!) so I wouldn't get too attached to it. The vase now sits proudly on Marcy's fireplace mantel, and she says it's one of her favorite things. I have also bought many purses, trinkets, and fancy hats, and toys for a dollar or two that have made a few little girls and boys very happy. I can give them for no particular occasion because they haven't set me back a week's pay, and it's amazing how much joy can be gotten with so little money.

I keep friends and family in mind the same way they think of me, and we are able to share not only the purchases, but also the idea that we think of each other and take the time to know each other's tastes and preferences. Finding the right gift for a person is not so tough, and it certainly has its rewards. By the way, I am still looking for Mr.

Wright, so if you find him in your travels, I'll be more than happy to work out a trade.

The Obsessive Collector

One of one is just one. Two of one is a pair. Three is a collection and four is the road to obsession.

Where to Thrift Shop

Thrift Shops

There are a variety of places to search for your valued treasures. Open-air sales, such as garage, tag, or barn-style sales, may be seasonal if you live in a state that has winter. Warmer climates have private outdoor sales going on all year, to the point where, as in Phoenix, there is a limit to the amount of sales each household may have in one year. In colder climates, outdoor bargain shopping begins in the spring and will continue through the fall. The outdoor sales will increase as the weather gets warmer, and you must take advantage of the multitudes while you can. Once the winter sets in, you should seek indoor flea markets, church sales, tag sales, or established charitable thrift and con-signment shops. The pickings may be slimmer, but the turnover is constant. If you frequent these places, you will eventually find your bargains.

Thrift and consignment shops are a good place for the beginner to start. They can usually be

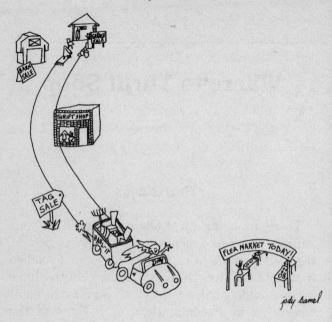

found in or near any sizable city or town. Prices
are pretty firm and marked on the merchandise,
and there's no rush to sift frantically through the
goods to get the best pick. Occasionally you will
see someone holding something you wish you had
gotten to first, but for the most part you can
browse leisurely. You will often find collectibles,
glassware, dishes, costume jewelry, accessories,
furniture, and vintage or new clothing—all waiting for a facelift and a new home. Old styles in all
these things always come around again, so you
must learn to spot the terrific original styles that

inspired the new versions; some originals are valuable in and of themselves. For instance, the 1950s television discarded in favor of the new wide screen may be a castoff to its first owner, but it is a real find for a smart kitsch collector. It could be a hot addition to a contemporary bedroom, but needs to be seen this way in the eye of the beholder. Until we have developed your imagination and your design and resource skills, thrift shops should provide enough of a selection for you to begin honing your bargain-spotting ability. Along with the old and carefully used, here you will often find merchandise that is still brand new, with tags still on it. Remember that sundress your daughter got in January, when she was eighteen months old, but didn't quite grow into by June? It may be hanging here in perfect condition waiting for a rightful owner. How about those wedding gift multiples? Aunt Anna's wineglass set may be in its original box on a shelf at the Salvation Army.

Look for thrift-shop locations in the yellow or white pages of the phone book. I do this in any city I travel to, and find different desirables according to the area. Arizona and California may have clay and terra-cotta pottery, while New York might have china and stemware. Different lifestyles require diverse household goods and clothing; there is no need to limit your search to sales just around your corner. The Salvation Army, St. Vincent De Paul, Goodwill, American Cancer Society, Veterans Association, Friends of Animals, churches, and charitable organizations have stores in most fairly well-populated towns.

Churches and hospitals frequently have thrift shops on their premises, but their hours may be limited. I find that church and temple shops often sell merchandise that is well cleaned and cared for because the parishioners take the time and trouble to make everything saleable. Call for directions and hours, and ask the thrift shops what days donations are accepted, to help you get best pick of the goods. Inquire also if they know of other thrift shops to direct you to. If you are at home or traveling, look in the newspaper for possible church sales and bazaars on the days you will be able to attend. Find addresses, get your map, and go. The more places you are aware of, the more chance you'll have to find the bargains. If there is a thrift shop en route to one of your destinations, you can plan a short detour for a quick look-see. Some of the best purchases are made in a minute on an unscheduled stop.

My friend Lois and I once took a trip to visit my family, and instead of taking the highways, we took my dad's suggestion and traveled the more scenic rural route. A five-hour drive turned into an eleven-hour shopping spree; we found church sales, garage sales, a fabulous wicker store, and an incredible auctioneer's warehouse where we filled up the car for thirteen dollars. I bought a deco chromium floor lamp for $3 (I rewired it myself) and spent two days removing the rust until it gleamed. A month later, we saw the identical lamp at a fancy antiques store with a price tag of $300! Lois's finds included a set of depression-glass cup-and-sandwich dish sets that she picked up for fifty cents a piece. I am not exaggerating when I tell you we saw the same dishes that summer at an open-air antiques show, priced at sixty dollars for a set of six. Great bargains are found, not born. I would like to mention that I attend the antiques shows not only to gloat over my successes, but also to learn and determine values. Knowledge always helps you sort out the junk from the jewels, and the rip-offs from the bargains. We will touch on sources of knowledge and developing an eye for good merchandise later on in this book. For now, I must still enlighten you on more sources for shopping.

Consignment Shops

Consignment shops are thrift shops that accept merchandise to be resold but must share the profit with the donor. The person making the donation waits for the item to sell and then receives a preset remuneration, while the shop takes its profit over and above this sum. Many consignment shops work on a percentage such as sixty percent of the selling price to the shop and forty percent to the contributor of the goods. This will sometimes make the prices slightly higher than other thrift stores, with less bargaining room for the buyer because there is more than one party involved in the money to be made. Some consignment shops buy their goods outright for resale and simply sell them. I find that in most consignment shops the merchandise is usually well screened and fairly well cleaned prior to reaching the selling floor.

Consignment shops may be run by charitable organizations as well as private individuals. Thrift shops may also work on a consignment basis, and these two types of stores can be profit or nonprofit. Consignment shops often have names such as "Nearly New" and "Second Time Around" and are usually listed in the yellow pages either under "Thrift Shops" or directly under the heading of "Consignment Shops." I find most consignment shops to be slightly better organized than regular thrift stores, but I am sure there are exceptions I haven't visited yet. A few consignment shops will have specialties, such as children's wear, evening wear, or designer clothing. In Los Angeles, I have heard tell of a consignment shop specializing in accepting donations from the stars for resale to ordinary folk like you and me. I have been unable to locate it as yet, but you can be sure I will do a thorough search during my next visit.

Consignment shops may also be an excellent way of reselling your own unwanted clothes and household goods. Just remember to keep records of what you gave to whom and periodically check the shops to see if your things have been sold. Shopkeepers usually have records of your saleables, but they don't always keep track of who gets their money, so you must do it yourself. Whenever I have given clothes to consignment shops, I have neglected to follow up on my money due; in my case it is better to donate them to charitable organizations and take the receipt for the tax write-off at the end of the year. It may not amount to much, but it makes sense to donate goods to the next person who may need them.

Estate Sales and Auction Warehouses

Estate sales began long ago when auctioneers would purchase entire households and auction off the contents. The word "estate" would connote expensive, antique, well-to-do. Today it may have the same meaning in some cases, but it has mostly come to indicate simply a lifetime accumulation. I don't know about you, but I can accumulate incredible amounts of stuff over short periods of time: The thought of a lifetime accumulation is mind boggling. I always wonder what kind of an estate sale my grandchildren will have someday of my hoards of stuff. They'll probably have piles of paraphernalia inside and out with hundreds of thrift shoppers wandering about saying, "What a bunch of junk!" Estate sales may still have fine antiques, but chances are they will be mixed with

a variety of many collectibles, appliances, outdoor
furniture, and other household goods. You can go
to estate sales at the homes of the original owners,
much as you would attend a yard or tag sale. The
area the sale is held in may tell you something
about the contents: Wealthy neighborhoods buy
expensive things and will command high prices for
often excellent-quality purchases. Don't be afraid
to go to these sales, just be aware. Older neighborhoods may have antiques and collectibles, and
newer ones may have more current merchandise,
such as baby supplies, tools, and housewares.

There are also auction houses that purchase
these estate contents and store them stockroom-
style for selling before and after the actual auction. At times only the leftovers from the auctions
will be stored for resale. If you are lucky, you will
happen upon a true junkman who buys entire lots
and sells the leftovers cheap. Since everyone's
knowledge and desires are different, even the best
auctioneer may have overlooked some choice
things that a smart thrift shopper can pick up for
a song.

The auction warehouses I have been to are usually dirty, dingy, and in dissarray. They are
crammed and piled with anything from salt dishes
to refrigerators. Be prepared to dig into the worst
piles for the best finds. Sift through and return to
search again for things you may have missed the
first time around. Occasionally you will have to
purchase an entire lot of goods to get the piece you

want; this method of buying distracts the seller from the single piece you're really after and may actually be less expensive than haggling over the one item you are anxious to acquire. This is precisely what many dealers do to get a bargain on a prized possession. The lesson is this: Sometimes you have to buy the junk pile to own the gem.

Once, at a tag sale I bought two wool blazers, one black wool coat, one white leather shawl-collared jacket, and two 1940s wool suits. The suits were my original choice, but the woman wanted to sell the whole lot, so I bought it all for $32. Each of the suits cost from $25 to $35 to have professionally altered, but they were just my style and color and made from beautiful material as well. In order to buy such fine quality suits new, I would have had to pay $200 to $300 per suit. They were a great bargain; I have worn the suits a lot, and even the leather jacket once or twice. For the few dollars I spent per item, I have certainly gotten my money's worth. I am simply following what the auctioneers and dealers do by buying the whole for the part.

I had an acquaintance years ago who began his career using this method of buying entire estates, cellars, and garages. He would drive to farmhouses and other homes, offer to clean out their attics or cellars for a "lot price," and then haul away the entire contents. He would first peruse these cellars and attics for things of exceptional value, and then offer one price for the whole batch.

This tactic allowed him to conceal the fact that there was anything there of particular value to him. There's no stopping a creative buyer at any sale. Today my acquaintance is a well-respected Manhattan antiques dealer, while I am happy to remain just a travelin', treasure-hunting thrift shopper.

Garage, Yard, Lawn, and Barn Sales

You will find garage, yard, lawn, and barn sales listed in the Classified section of the newspaper or in your local shopping publication. They will be listed randomly throughout or, under headings such as "Merchandise Offerings," "Daily Shopper," "For Sale by Owner," "Auctions and Sales," etc. In some towns, however, you can just drive around and find a garage sale, lawn sale, or some such thing on every corner. Signs may be posted on poles and trees, indicating the date, time, and place of the sale. If the date is not posted, I usually do not try to find the sale; nine times out of ten the sign will be a leftover that a seller was just too lazy to take down. Please make a notation here if you are planning your own garage, tag, or lawn sale, remember that signs on the highway have to be read from a moving car! Make them clear, simple, and easily readable; and I beg you to remove them when the sale has ended, so that dedicated hunters like myself don't have to waste time and gas searching for the nonexistent sale.

Since these are outdoor sales, they may also be seasonal; bargain-shopping frenzy in areas with four seasons will have a late winter buildup before the spring break, which is then followed by the all-out summer fiesta. Private sales such as these are held on the lawns of private residences, lining neighborhood streets, or in driveways or parking lots, where one or a few families gather informally to sell their treasures.

Garage, yard, lawn, and barn sales have the unique benefit of almost endless space for the merchandise. This means serious digging and searching, but the results are often worth it. Items may escape being price-tagged at these sales, so feel free to handle, inspect, and ask questions. At times things do not get priced simply because the owner does not know what to ask, thus leaving the buyer an open invitation to make offers. Bear in mind that the goods at these sales were once the seller's treasures, before they were his or her junk, so be nice and courteous when picking through the piles and making an offer for purchase.

The basic goods selection rule for garage and other types of sales is as follows: If the sale begins at 9 A.M. and you arrive early, you will get the pick of the litter but at the highest price of the day. If you are willing to give up some of the pickings and attend later, you will get lower prices, with more bargaining power. You must go early if you desire the best selection. Antiques and consignment dealers do. They smell a good sale with a sixth sense acquired from experience, knowledge, and practice. They know where and how to buy as well as how to make a good deal. You will soon be able to buy with the best of them.

If you are very industrious, you may attend early to look over the booty, scout the prices, and return later to make the acquisition. You run the risk of losing your choices to other buyers, but if the prices are too high in the beginning, it may pay off in the end. My cousins Sandy and Tony went to an indoor/outdoor yard sale in Scottsdale, Arizona, where they saw a love seat with chaise for $850 and the matching sectional sofa for $750. They made their offers and were rejected, but returned later in the day to see that the pieces were still unsold. Once again they made an offer, which was also unaccepted. Undaunted, they returned to the scene of the sale shortly before its conclusion with *cash in hand* and succeeded in buying the love seat, chaise, and sectional sofa for a total of $750! Perseverance paid off, and showing the cash helped close the "buy." A little risky, perhaps, but even if they had lost out, there would always have been another sale tomorrow.

An interesting advantage to outdoor sales is that once you are more adept, you may learn to shop with your eyes as you pass by. Do not do this if you are the driver, but if you are the passenger your eyes are free to scope out the scene for objects of interest. Scan shopping is an important skill to practice and develop for going to sales crammed with goods. It is the art of perusing groups of merchandise quickly in search of the needle in the haystack. Collectors do this automatically, looking for their specific prized treasures, which they are already famililar with. If you are seeking something particular, such as a hedge clipper or a blender, scan shopping helps you spot it and grab it before the next browser sees it. I will discuss the subject of scan shopping in more detail when I explain the development of shopping skills. There are still a few sale sources to uncover before tackling techniques.

Tag Sales

Tag sales are a relatively new concept in the thrift-shopping scene. Outside and roadside sales can be traced back to fruit pushcarts, while shopping for used goods at a tag sale inside a residence is a more recent development, stemming from estate sales and auctions. Unlike open-air yard, lawn, garage, and barn sales, tag sales are usually inside a home, where everything for sale is tagged. Sound simple? The first time I took my friend Robyn to a tag sale, she was shocked and appalled that we were going *inside* the person's house. She had been to outdoor sales before but had never actually wandered around inside a stranger's home to look at personal possessions. Needless to say,

"He got that crown at a garage sale and
now he thinks he's *King of the Jungle!*"

twenty minutes later she was standing on a bath-
tub edge in a private privy marked with a "Do Not
Enter" sign, trying on belts and blouses. It only
proves that the fever is easy to catch. Easy to
catch, yes, but the great success stories come from
cultivation of the thrift-shopping art. Have no
fear, for you are reading your way to triumph!

At tag sales there are often rooms such as the
one Robyn invaded, with "Do Not Enter" signs
posted to tell browsers that there is nothing in
them for sale. Occasionally items will be separa-
tely marked "NFS" (Not For Sale), but everything
else is up for grabs. Once in a while there will be
some oversights in this department. While I was
in the process of purchasing three beach bags at a
tag sale in California, the lady who owned them
saw me paying for them at the designated cash-
ier's table and went into a veritable tizzy demand-
ing to know where I'd gotten them from and

insisting that they weren't supposed to be for sale. Believe me when I tell you I was *not* ransacking her closets. The bags were under an open shelf in the basement on which everything was for sale. A helper gave me a price, so I had no reason to believe these bags were not part of the pack. Of course, I relinquished them immediately, with some dismay at having practically been accused of poaching. I didn't want to cause a stir, because I rarely argue at a tag sale, or any kind of sale for that matter. If someone wants something so badly he or she can't live without it, I periodically give up my prize. I only give it up if the person is nice, honest, or hysterical, however.

I despise being conned, especially while shopping. Once at a weekend tag sale a woman insisted that she had seen first the children's blocks that I was holding in a box in my hands and that she had every intention of buying them. I had been carrying them around for a few minutes, and she was nowhere in sight when I had first picked them up. I explained to her that I was buying them as a gift. I hadn't seen anyone else looking at the blocks when I found them, and if she had picked them up, I certainly would not have taken them from her. Imagine two grown women arguing over blocks! She proceeded to rant and rave about wanting them herself, but she hadn't noticed them until I had them in my hands. This was surely one of those cases when she wished she had seen them first, but clearly had not. The woman then continued to follow me around the sale, badgering me along the way, but I bought the blocks and put them in my car before returning to shop some more. (I don't trust putting things down and having someone watch them before they are paid for, as they are invariably gone when you return to them. There is often a sneaky shopper waiting for this opportunity, so it is better to make a trip to the car and come back, rather than risk your treasure being snapped up while no one's looking.) When I came back into that sale, a man who had watched the whole thing told me the woman was a dealer and knew the value of the blocks I had bought for $4 to be about $75 and very desirable for resale. She was bothering me only because I had discovered a good find before she did, and her intention was to make a profit on the blocks. To backtrack to the actual point of this discourse: *Be nice.* You are in someone's home. Use your manners. Guests should still be respectful and polite, even if some of the buyers and sellers are lunatics. Nine times out of ten, nice works better than nasty. If the raving woman had been amicable, I probably would have given her the blocks. But some people just don't play nice.

Tag sales often sell most of the contents of the residence, including furniture, rugs, housewares, clothing, tools, and whatever else isn't nailed down. Bric-a-brac (an invented term meaning miscellaneous stuff) will be found at most sales and is usually scattered throughout the house. There will be tables and boxes full of these small trinkets and accessories that you will have to be willing to dig through. Tag sales are similar in wares to outdoor sales, except that the sellers don't move everything outside. Instead they let perspective buyers wander around their abode in search of the perfect bargain.

In some towns there are entrepeneurs whose business it is to conduct these sales for the sellers. They place ads in Classified sections and local newspapers with heading words like "Smasharoo" and "Blast" and "Better Sale." You will eventually be able to determine which tag sale consultants are conducting the sales; you will also come to learn just by reading their ads whose sales you want to attend and which to avoid.

In return for a commission on the day's take, tag-sale consultants are responsible for pricing and selling available paraphernalia. This practice may be beneficial to the thrift shopper because tag-sale consultants have no sentimental attachments that influence the prices. On the other hand, they are experienced at determining the actual resale value of merchandise, which may make it more difficult to pick up a real steal early in the day. Toward the end of the day, the consultants are more anxious to make a sale at almost any price (low commission is better than no commission), whereas the original owner remembering what was paid for it, how it was used, and all the good memories attached to it may have trouble parting with an item for a low price. It's not unlike the way you'll keep an old sweatshirt or sneakers too long because you're so used to having them around—well loved, hard to part with. A tag-sale consultant prefers to make the sale. Once again, I remind you to be nice. These consultants get battered all day by bargain hunters, and that is not an easy position to be in. Be fair when you make your offers and you will often come out ahead. Don't offer $2 for a Louis XIV settee and expect to get it. (Although sometimes a low offer is better than no offer.) I personally believe that there should still be some ethics even when you are negotiating for a steal. There's a steal, and then there's stealing.

Getting a "steal" is when you buy a great item for an excellent price. "Stealing" is when you knowingly swindle someone out of a valuable piece. Some people believe this is part of what great thrift-shopping successes are made of: I cannot say they are wrong, I can only say that there are times when it doesn't feel quite right. A few summers back I had called a tag-sale consultant that mentioned an Eames rocker in their ad, as well as a phone number at which to contact the seller. When I called to inquire about the price, the woman said a dealer had offered her $40 for the chair. This angered me because I was certain the dealer knew the real value of the chair and was trying to take monumental advantage of the situation. A profit on the resale could have still been realized, even if she had offered the owner $100 for the chair. The dealer was just being greedy. Sight unseen, I told the owner I would give her $70 (even if it wasn't in great shape), knowing it was a more fair offer because the chair was worth a few hundred dollars (especially if it were in mint condition). When I went to see the chair, I discovered it to be perfect: leather-upholstered, with wood rockers; small and beautiful. The owner proceeded to show me photos of herself rocking her son in the very same chair. Her son was grown now and getting married a few weeks from that day. I asked her if her son wanted the chair, because this was truly an item to be handed down in a family. She said he had no interest in it, but I mentioned that perhaps her future daughter-in-law might want this heirloom. We decided that she would inquire and get back to me. As it turned out, her daughter-in-law-to-be was thrilled to have the chair for the future grandchildren, and the owner thanked me profusely for being so honest. I didn't get the chair, but she did sell me a Russel Wright plastic dinnerware set that I treasure to this day.

By the way, last year I bought my own Eames chair at the Salvation Army for $3. It was tagged low because of its poor condition. It was in need of major repair, and wasn't as desirable as the

rocker, but I felt I had gotten my reward for a good
deed. I'm sure there are lots of people who would
say I was crazy to screw up my original bargain,
and they may be right. But you win some, you lose
some, and the beauty of it is there will always be
another chance to strike a fair deal. And if you're
out there, Mrs. Bodner, I have a feeling you're tell-
ing your grandchildren this same story.

Bazaars and Rummage Sales

Bazaars and rummage sales are "mixed bag"
sales held by churches, temples, and charitable organizations. By "mixed bag" I mean that they have
old and new merchandise, all usually donations
given by the organization's constituents. These
sales are often held in the meeting room or enter-
tainment hall of the organization's building, and
tend to have lots of stuff piled up and set out. I
find the prices to be exceptionally cheap, but you

have to be in the mood to dig at these functions. I don't find real treasures here, but I usually come out with a doodad or two. Few people donate things of real value in the collectible or antiques categories for these sales, but housewares, clothing, and small appliances often abound. If there is a raffle being held, for a new television or other such item, I always buy a ticket but never win. I'm certain someone is awarded the prize, even if it isn't me, and I always console myself with home-made cookies from the bake sale if they are having one. There may also be a mailing list to sign on to, to keep abreast of future sales. Otherwise, watch for advertising in the classifieds or local newsletters to track down bazaars and rummage sales. Also, check community news boards in supermarkets and organizations to keep abreast of these events.

Flea Markets

Today's flea markets are often prearranged parking lots full of regular vendors selling off-price new merchandise. There are still a few, however, that will be large lots where anyone can show up for the day and pay for their space. At these flea markets, you will find a mixture of junk and antiques along with spaces for new merchandise. These are essentially like a multi-family sale; people come and sell whatever they have to get rid of.

You can peruse the rows and see all types of buys. Some will be bargains, some will not. The standard buying rules apply here. If you attend early in the day, you will get the best pickings but at the highest prices. If you go midday or later, make sure to take note of whether people are walking around with purchases. If they aren't, you may have lots of bargaining leeway. Also, most folks don't want to have to repack all their stuff, so at the end of the day, goods go for cheap. I often find great toys, clothes, and housewares at these flea markets, along with jewelry, accessories, and tools. Furniture is not always the favorite item to bring, because people may not be willing to lug big pieces to a flea market and then possibly have to lug them back home. If there is furniture you want, make your offers. But be prepared to take it then and there.

Many flea markets are open every weekend. The location remains the same, but the vendors change weekly. I like these a lot because if you know where these flea markets are every weekend, you can pop in without much planning. It may not seem adventuresome, but there is usually a thing or two worth buying. Even if there isn't, it's fun browsing on a nice day. To find the times and locations for these flea markets, refer again to the local classifieds and shopping newspapers, or ask friends in different towns if they know of any good markets to attend. Some weeks may have better sellers than others, so don't be discouraged if at first you don't succeed. Try, try again.

Multi-Family Garage Sales

Multi-family garage sales take two forms: One is a group of families putting their goods together at one person's yard or garage, and the other is a series of sales in the same neighborhood, with lots of families holding their own. When a group of families show at one place, there will be a good mixture of buyables for an assortment of tastes. The goods are usually lettered or numbered, so each seller knows which stuff belongs to whom. When you've chosen your purchase, you must seek out the seller and do your bargaining and purchasing directly. At the most recent multi-family sale of this type that I attended, I bought a shower curtain for seventy-five cents from one lady and a pair of almost new Frye boots for $3 from another. The boots belonged to a young woman whose mother was also participating in the sale, and they proceeded to have an argument about them. "I paid almost $200 for those!" said the mother. "I bought them for you in Southampton at a very exclusive store!" "But, Mom," the daughter replied, "I never wore them because they didn't fit!" The mother went on to insist that three dollars was a ridiculous amount to get for them and claimed she would wear them herself rather than sell them at that price. As the daughter began to remind her that they weren't even close to her size, I paid my three bucks and got the heck out of there with my bargain.

The other type of multi-family sale I mentioned involves an entire neighborhood throwing individual sales all in the same locale. Usually there will be a map at each sale showing where the other sales are being held, and you can take a walk from one to the next or drive around if the distances are too great. I enjoy these sales because there will always be a multitude of merchandise, due to the sheer number of families who dig out their salables from all corners of their homes. You never feel as if you're missing a bargain, because if one or two sales don't pan out, there is another one to be reckoned with just around the corner. It's a delightful day trip for the true thrift-shopping sportsman or sportswoman.

Map of Multi-Family Garage Sales

This map was available at each sale. I found the ad for this multi-family sale in the Classified section of a local daily newspaper. I was unfamiliar with the town, but no need to worry. Armed with the ad and my trusty map, I located the first sale, picked up this map, and continued to all the sales marked.

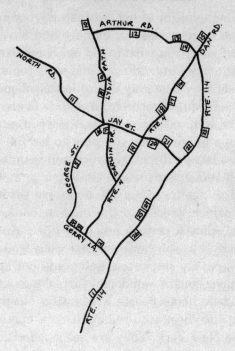

Auctions

Auctions are birds of a different feather. On the selling floor, the pace is fast and furious. It's a little intimidating, but if you go in with a little knowledge as ammunition, you will feel more confident about participating in the fun. Advertised auctions almost always list an inspection period preceeding the sale. I cannot stress enough the importance of looking at goods as closely as possible before stepping in to bid. At inspection you may examine merchandise for damage and have time to select what you wish to bid on. Some items go up on the block individually, and some come up in groups or lots. A lot may be a collection of one type or just a boxful of goods to be sold. Lots are numbered or lettered for inspection, so you must be conscious of which lot you plan to bid on. Some auctions have a directory which will help you follow the auctioneer's track. On larger or more desirable things there may be a reserve set by the seller, which precludes the auction house from selling below a certain accepted price. Auctions are tricky, but you can score extremely well if you are aware. My stepsister, Kelly, and her spouse, Ray, have bought wonderful furnishings at auction. Their home boasts a beautiful sleigh bed, rocker, and chest acquired at farmers' auctions in upstate New York. They are seasoned attendees who have gotten over "auction fever," which is a common problem novices face.

Auction fever commences when the bidding reaches a frenzy, and it is easy to get caught up and lose sight of your original intentions. My best advice is to determine your top price before the bid and don't exceed it. My second-best advice is to attend an auction or two without bidding, to get the feel for the way they work. Auctions are well attended by experienced bidders and dealers. Your chances are as good as theirs at picking up bargains, but be knowledgeable about what you're bidding on and don't get sucked into the bidding floor for more than you can handle. If you have made a successful bid, it is usually required that you pay in full and pick up your purchase at the end of the auction. Sometimes someone will bring the purchase to your seat, trusting you to put up full remuneration at the end. Some auction houses require a deposit before bidding, but you are generally still responsible for full payment and removal of your purchases. Ask the rules at the beginning so there will be no surprises. If you plan to buy big, bring an appropriate hauling vehicle as cash-and-carry is the general rule.

There are a few pitfalls involved in this kind of secondhand buying, but the rewards are great if you prepare properly. The best preparation is knowing the value of the goods. This is not easy for most of us, so follow your instincts and don't let your emotions override your head. Big items require research. A ten-dollar bid on a chair that turns out to be junk might not be a big deal, but a large bid on an antique armoire should be made only after careful consideration. There are auctions today that include everything from books to cars and even homes. Auto and home auctions are a specialized field altogether and should be approached only after extensive research. I have attended some of these auctions myself, but there are legal and financial implications involved the explanation of which would require my writing an entirely separate book. I prefer to stick to the movable things slightly bigger than a bread box, with price tags that don't require loans.

Shopping the Street for Free

It has been said that the best things in life are free. When it comes to the ultimate bargain, this is also the case. Someday I vow to buy a van so I can stuff my car full of things found put out at the curb. Once, my dad was out walking our dog and spotted a music stand out at the curb, destined for the dump. Its wood top was in perfect shape, although the iron three-legged stand was a little rusty. After some diligent cleaning, the stand looked as beautiful as the day it was bought, and it still sits on my stair landing with a stately old dictionary perched on it. Even with today's thoughts on recycling, it is often difficult or expensive for people to have furniture carted away; rather than pay to have it removed, they will put it out at the curb in hopes that someone will pick it up. In fact, a friend told me of her neighbor who tried to strike a bargain at a garage sale; the seller wouldn't take a lower price, but the next day the buyer drove past the house and saw the item she had tried to purchase put out to trash. If you feel odd about just helping yourself, you can always knock on the door and inquire, but it is usually unnecessary to do so. I have listened to tales of tables with chairs, wood chests, and assorted furniture acquired for free. A glass table and chairs I heard of were stumbled upon by a young man who drives an ice-cream truck. He saw the table at the curb with four matching Breuer-type chairs, and without even thinking, he loaded them onto his truck. He then cut his route short and appeared at his girlfriend's new apartment with a fabulous housewarming gift. The odds are against these great finds on the street, but you can increase your chances by learning when "spring cleanups" and large pickups are scheduled for a particular town. Ask residents you are acquainted with or call the town halls to find this information, and then use it well.

My friend Robyn (the one we introduced to tag sales) has a mom who knows that in a certain suburb on Long Island you can put out any size item for trash pickup on Thursday. On Wednesday evening she gets her station wagon out and cruises around this well-to-do neighborhood, picking up excellent chests of drawers, chairs, and end tables, discarded at the curb. If the use or condition of the item is questionable, she will pick it up anyway and inspect it later. The curb isn't the only place I've heard tell of shopping for free; there have been many success stories told about Dumpster rescues. I know of a man who picked up oak office furniture, complete with files and shelves, and built an office at home virtually for free. He found them in the Dumpster behind a bank just after they had remodeled.

A lovely woman I spoke to on the phone a few times told me her dishwasher was gotten off the street for free after someone who was remodeling put it out for trash pick-up. She said the contractor who was working at her own house saw it, picked it up, and installed it in her kitchen. Last I heard, it was still going strong.

My most recent free acquisition was an old pine chest someone discarded. It has hinges and a flap for a padlock, with some lieutenant's address and an old railway sticker on it. I originally used it in the store I work in, as a prop to dress up an antique vignette. My boss wanted to know why I had brought in that beat-up old box, but a week later someone tried to buy it! I almost sold it for $200 but decided I needed it at home to store my sheets and towels. I used a good wood cleaner on it, followed by some Old English scratch cover, and it looks fabulous. I have begun to notice these kinds of trunks in antiques stores, and I haven't found one yet for under $250!

When shopping for free, it's difficult to loiter, so I find it is best to "take it now and discard or donate it later." It is not likely that you will be able to set out saying to yourself, "Tonight I'm looking for an armoire"; it's merely an adventure to see what's out there. Is it tough to do this in the dark? Yes, but when it is light out it is fun to cruise for cache without cash. The question is: Can shopping without spending money really be called shopping? Or is it just "eventful browsing"? Whatever it is called, you can't beat the thrill of the conquest without currency.

---------------------------------✂---------------------------------

How to Thrift Shop:
Thrift-Shopping Strategies

How to Attend the Most
Secondhand Sales
in the Least Amount of Time

"On Saturday mornings, Doreen and I leave the
kids with our husbands and go sale-ing. We only
have an hour and a half so we've got to keep our
bargain hunting short and sweet. We plan our
strategy the night before for maximum results."
—Marcy

Successful thrift shopping requires a bit of organization. Once you have found ads for thrift
stores, auctions, and private sales in your local
newspapers and phone books, you need to spend
just a minute to organize your shopping. Thrift
stores will have specific weekly hours, so you can
fit those in at convenient times. Auctions may last
an hour or a few, so you may only attempt to go to
one on any given day. Garage, yard, tag, and barn
sales happen sporadically, so it will take a bit

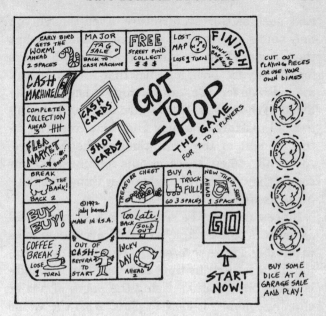

more planning to cover a few of them at a time. It's relatively easy to do; after you've done it once or twice, it only takes a few minutes to save a lot of time and confusion.

Learning to read between the lines in the classified ads for these sales is your best shortcut to success. Knowing what is implied will help direct you to the sales worth attending. For instance, if a sale ad touts "Thomasville furniture," you know you will find mostly traditional, conservative goods. An ad that states "depression glass" means there may be other items from that same time pe-

riod, such as thirties furniture. Even though you
may not be interested in the glass, you might want
the furniture from the same era that may be there
for the buying. Look for clues that what you seek
may also be for sale, even though it isn't actually
listed. If the ad says "fifties furniture" and you collect old toasters, you may find some from the fifties, bought at the same time as the furniture.
After all, when these people purchased their
couch, they probably bought other things for their
home as well.

Since sales may be scattered all around, I will
sometimes pick a single area and cover a few sales
in one day. I have covered a lot of ground by group-
ing the sales first by time and day, then by neighborhood and location. Using the pages of ads or
clippings makes it easy to plan. With the whole
page in front of you, use medium-blue ink or any
contrasting color to circle the sales you are interested in. I use medium blue because you can write
right over the copy and make pertinent notes next
to the ads. I note the day and times and, in con-
junction with a good map, the map grid location of
the sale. Thus, even while driving, I can leave the
map page open and clearly see where I should be.
Sometimes I write simple directions, especially if
I'm going to a few sales in an unfamiliar area.

Consulting a map is important if you want to
cover a lot of ground. While I consult the map, I
check which sales I should go to first and in what

order; I then number each sale, picking the first, second, third, and so on that will allow the shortest travel with the most stops in the least time.

Another variation of this method is to cut out each ad and paste or tape it onto a sheet of paper, with notes to the side of each. Whatever method works for you will help you get the most out of your time. I only wish I could be this organized with everything!

Once you have done some thrift shopping with planning, you will learn from looking which neighborhoods have what kinds of goods, and you will become more adept at picking which sales to head for. Some towns have older collectibles and antiques, while others will have more current clothes and housewares. Even if you don't buy, always be sure to observe. Take notice of the type of merchandise, styles, and quality found in each area you shop. A pattern or time period will often recur for particular neighborhoods. Builders who constructed groups of homes often filled them with families within a relatively short time span. If families moved into a community together, the things they bought will have similarities in style and material. Observation will make for future success!

merchandise for sale

HOME FURNISHINGS AND SALES

BR SET. Mahogany 1930's style includes full size mattress with nitestands Call eves 000-0000

BR SET. king size waterbed with platform. Waveless with healer. Like new! 000-0000

COUCH, Blue floral contemp with matching chair. Paid $800 Must Sell. 000-0000

TAG SALE
DAGWOOD PARK-contents of estate-furn, art, collectibles, glassware,tools. Garage full of bric-a-brac. Cash only. 4/4 and 4/5 9-5. No earlybirds. 00 Arin Lane off Rte. 16

IN ROOM. Thomasville-like new fruitwood, table, 6 chairs and hutch. Asking $500 Call 000-000

HOME FURNISHINGS AND SALES

GREAT RIVER "BETTER SALE"
14 Manor Dr. E. 4/3& 4/4 9-3 all contents of designer home incl leath sofas, French trunks, Donia Dinette, crystal,statue, set, artwork grand baby wicker, etc.

TAG SALE
GR. RIVER WATERFRONT
FRI. 4/3 SAT. 4/4 8-4
Fabulous furnishings, furs & household goods. Leath sofa, oak armoire, brass bed, figurines, silver, Wedgewood, video equip, tools . State pkwy to Exit 12 to Beach Rd. to River Way #00

GARAGE AND MOVING SALE--moving out of state, must sell all contents. All Offers. Call for appt 000-0000

HOME FURNISHINGS AND SALES

LIDO WEST MOVING SALE. Fri.4/3-Sun. 4/5 9am Everything must go. Collector art, china, books, crystal, record collection, grand E.P.O.

FURNITURE, 3pcs.mint, blue & mauve floral, orig. 3k. Will sell $800. 000-0000

LI RM Col. like new, 5pcs incl end tsbles and tea cart. Teak with custom fabric. 000-0000

LR SET. din rm set, two bed rooms, VCR, CD play, eves only 000-0000

MASTER BEDROOM. Black style Grey set. Reasonable. 000-0000 eves & wkends.

LONG ACRE SELLOUT!
00 Longdon Ct. Sat. Sun. 9-4

HOME FURNISHINGS AND SALES

MOORVILLE BLAST!!!
Collector selling all. Oriental rugs china, books, jewelry, fabric, trunks, sofas, carts, chairs, br sets, dining room, figurines, crystal & more! Cash & carry Sun. 4/5 only. Jode La. (Hwy 66, Exit 7, Left on Jim Rd. Rt. on Jode)

MOORVILLE GARAGE SALE. Baby items, memorabilia, furn and kitch set. Baseball cards, Barbies, maternity clothes. Crater Ct. at East end. 4/5 9-3

MURPHY BED 100" CUSTOM Dark wood with all built ins. Can be cut to fit. Paid $3000. Best offer 000-0000.

GARAGE SALE SUN. 9-2 NORWOOD- 0 Eldon Crs. 10-4 Hutch, modualr sofa, ottoman,

...Eames chairs, ... stereo. all MINT!! ... coffee table, Eames ... prints. Make offers. 000-0000

DREAMVILLE SMASH
At Green Estates 0 Lum Dr. 9-5 Sat. 4/4. Magnificent desk and breakfront, dining set, TV, 50 yr accumulation. Must sell this weekend! Garage full incl 1982 Cadillac.

EAST ELLIS SALE
House full of household items and asst collectibles. 4/3, 4/4, 4/5 8-6. Cedar St. off Maple Ave.

FURNISHINGS : 30-60' BR sofa, den sofas, chests, chairs, lamps, old quilts, fabrics, tools and clothing. Call Eves 000-0000.

FURNITURE FOR SALE-like new. Dining set, LR BR and Wash/Dry. Cheap. 000-0000

GARAGE SALE-50 yrs of all kinds of antique. 4/4 9-4 Cash only off 8th St. Elmwood

GARAGE SALE
00 Old Mill Rd.-Tons of mint cond clothing, housewares & furniture. Custom sofas, TVs, piano, china. Sat. & Sun. 9-? Sal St. to Valley to Old Mill.

HAMMOND ORGAN, banjo, drum set for sale. Excel. Call eves and weekends 000-0000

KIRKTOWN- Huge collection of misc. furn incl. sofas, tables, dinette, lawn mower, appliances, rugs and more. Cash & carry. 0 Lind Dr. bet. Fult St. & Deva Rd. 4/4, 4/5

KITCHEN SET brass & glass w/ cantilever breuer chairs. Paid $400. Best offer over 200. Days 000-0000

KITCHEN CABINETS never used. 6' upper & lower w/ dw, GE fridge. 000-0000

KLARKSON- Garage Sale Fri. & Sat. 10-16—toys, baby items, records, dishes, 55 gal. fish tank, twin bunk beds, etc. 00 Duke Rd. Bet Fent St. and Bet La.

LIDO BLAST
Sat. 4/4, 9am-4pm 0 Dud La. Huge asst from Granma's attic. Clothing, Jewelry, frames, furs, clocks,

LONG ACRE GOODIE!
Selling all contents. Junk to jewels. Dealers welcome. 4/3, 4/4 9-3pm

LONG BEACH
Tons of collectibles & junque for everyone. Tools, bottles, glass, Louis IV club chair..mica BR's, ladies clothing, toys, crib, desk, file cab, mower, grill. Fri. thru Sun. 10am-4pm. No earlybirds.

GARAGE SALE
LONG BEACH HULLABALLOO Wicker, fixtures, fans, clothes, rugs, office furn, tables, sofas, mattresses, king br set, bar, kitch set, riding mower, patio set. 0 Acre ct. 4/5 9-3pm

LONG BEACH-00 Bayway 9-3 Fri. & Sat. 4/3, 4/4. Gym equip. gas dryer, cane chairs, Russel Wright china, dehumidifier, kit/garden needs. Aura Rd. to Sot St. to Bayway.

MOVING SALE-designer furn & access. Villa sofas, Eta tables, brass etagere, clothing, VCR, wide screen TV. Call 000-0000

NORTH ISLAND- Garage Sale Everything and the kitchen sink! Garden, office, den and patio furn. Craft items, reali... lamps, end tables, low price. Main St. to First to...

OSTEP COVE Full tag... Fully ... appliances... quality exc... Rd. Bikes, piano, wind... linens, etc. Call for add'l...

OAK KITCHEN SET ... in 2 car... top 42"... Cal...

PANASONIC ... old perfect working ... with outdoor cover ... mower w/ mulch ...

TAG SALE BLASTER!!!
PLAINVILLE - Rocky Rd. 4/5 9-6 and 4/12 9-6. Don't miss it! Designer furnishings, antique clock collection, dolls, secretary, 1920's depression glass, headboard, sideboard, console, server, BR sets, LR sofas, Victorian chests, chairs and sewing tables.

TAG SALE
GR. RIVER WATERFRONT
FRI. 4/3 SAT. 4/4 8-4

Fabulous furnishings, furs & household goods. Leath sofa, oak armoire, brass bed, figurines, silver, Wedgewood, video equip, tools. State pkwy to Exit 12 to Beach Rd. to River Way #00.

GARAGE SALE

00 Old Mill Rd.--Tons of mint cond clothing, housewares & furniture. Custom sofas, TV's, piano, china. Sat. & Sun. 9-4. Sal St. to Valley to Old Mill.

GARAGE SALE--50 yrs of all kinds of antiques. 4/4 9-4 Cash only. 0 W. 8th St. Elmwood.

LIDO WEST MOVING SALE

Fri. 4/3-Sun. 4/5 9am-5pm Everything must go! Curirios, art, china, books, records, sectional gas grill. 000 Este Dr.

---

① 25A TO RT. ON CENTERPORT RD.

} 25A/E PAST DELI TO TOWN HALL LFT AFTER TOWN HALL

③A BACK TO 25 W. TO SWALLOW RD. TO 8TH

④ ? RT. 11 W. TO DEB 4A. TO HARRIS TO ESTE

LONG BEACH

Tons of collectibles & junque for everyone. Tools, bottles, glass, Louis IV club chair, mica BR's, ladies clothing, toys, crib, desk, file cab, mower, grill. Fri. thru Sun. 10am-4pm. No earlybirds.

LONG BEACH-00 Bayway 9-3 Fri. & Sat. 4/3, 4/4. Gym equip., gas dryer, cane chairs. Russel Wright china, dehumidifier, kit/garden needs. Aura Rd. to Set St. to Bayway.

GARAGE SALE SUN. 9-2

NORWOOD- 0 Eldon Crs. 10-4
Hutch, modular sofa, ottoman, bunk beds, IBM pc, dishes, microwave, upright freezer, Doulton, stereo. all MINT!

---

① ?. NEAR HIGH SCHOOL - SIGNS UP

② 25A TO CHURCH TO HIGHLAND TO BAYWAY

③ RTE 11 TO MAIN TO PYRES TO ELDON

Scanning, Searching, and Digging

"Dig into the messiest box in the dirtiest corner.
Chances are, no one has looked through it yet."
                                        —Roxanne

Now that you've figured out where you're going,
its time to learn *how* to look. Basically you will do
three things: scan, search around, and finally dig
through the hidden corners. On your first approach to any sale, you should take a broad look
at the merchandise to see if anything catches your
eye right off the bat. Collectors do this automatically in search of their prized pieces. Even if you
are not a collector, you can scan the area, shelves,
or tables for anything of interest to you. In retail
training seminars, I learned that when a customer
enters a store, it only takes fifteen seconds for him
or her to scan an entire department. People do this
inadvertently; remember to use this technique to
your advantage at thrift sales and stores. If you
need a blender and you see one that looks good,
pick it up right away and continue scanning. It is
important to actually pick up anything you may
want, before another buyer spots it. Possession is
nine-tenths of the law, so you need to have any
possible purchase in your hands before the next
shopper decides he or she wants it and picks it up
in *his or her* hands.

On the next pass, you will do a more thorough search. Move things around, look behind objects, pick up and inspect markings, materials, size, and any other pertinent details. A closer look at a rack of clothing may get you a nice wool sweater you had previously overlooked. Check what you have in your hands and see if there are irregularities. Maybe the blender you whisked up has no lid; perhaps the sweater has a snag, and you won't use it. Be certain, however, because once you have put it down, it becomes anybody's fair game.

The last look is the dig. That box in the corner under the table that looks ignored may have a buried treasure in it. An uninviting appearance often dissuades folks from touching, but it never stops the dedicated digger. Look through clothing racks hanger by hanger to make sure you haven't missed that suede skirt that wasn't level with the other hangers. Move bric-a-brac on shelves and tables to find what's hiding in the back. At a thrift store recently I found a box of ugly white dishes, but upon removing the dishes and looking further, I discovered some lovely glasses from the thirties beneath them at the bottom of the box. Don't be afraid to get dirty: carry some wipes in your car, pocket, or purse for a simple way to wash up after touching everything.

Chances are you will sometimes pick up some useless junk among your purchases. It is difficult to tell if an item is worth having or will end up a waste of money. Ask yourself if you need or want an item, or plan to give it as a gift. If not, don't bring it home unless it's so cheap you can't resist. Don't fret over the mistakes that aren't costly. To avoid the big errors, it is imperative that you develop an eye for quality and value. Frequenting sales will teach you to do this just by trial and error, but it's easy to sharpen your skills by allowing your brain to do its job.

Using Your Powers of Observation: How to Identify Quality and Value

"Don't tell anyone where you got it. You're supposed to like the finer things in life."
—Mom Bamel

I do like the finer things in life! That doesn't mean they have to be new. I would rather have an old sofa of quality than a new couch that is poorly made. That is one of the reasons why thrift shopping has become so popular. As we exited the excessive eighties, we ran into a recession. Our tastes had improved, while our pocketbooks became less full. A well-made blazer or a quality chair will remain so forever. If kept in good condition, quality goods will be as beautiful now as they were then. Quality is timeless. An acquaintance of mine buys old men's suits for about $10 each and then spends $30 to have them fitted for herself. Talk about impeccably dressed! Her secret is spotting fine fabrics and making them fit her style. A suit like this, new, from a department store, with a designer label, no doubt would cost hundreds. Value and quality are things we already know; we just need to put our knowledge to work.

I am fortunate that I am able to notice trends. I am not psychic, just observant. When bell bottoms began their comeback, I spotted them sparsely in ladies' fashion magazines. Knowing the era they came from and having actually been there to see it, I knew it was only a matter of time before platform shoes and crazy pocketbooks would follow. Now, I may not wear bell bottoms again, but I was able to snap up some great platform shoes and wonderful inexpensive, original pocketbooks before everyone else was shopping the trend. You don't necessarily need firsthand knowledge of an era to find out what comes along with it, however. Old movies, television shows, or books and magazines will tell you what trends are coming, after you've seen the initial indicators. Furniture, housewares, artwork, and many of the material things of an era will often return to popularity all together. Clothing style is one of the easiest ways to spot a trend coming. Rent a movie from the time period of the style or take out a book. I took out an old Barbra Streisand movie when I saw bell bottoms reappearing, and I discovered big flowered dresses, colorful headgear, and the platform shoes that would go with it. Before the trend hit full force, I had already purchased my platforms, zebra boots, and bags when the price was still low and the quality pickings were available, before everyone else took notice.

The most difficult problem I have when I wear those "height of fashion" finds is how to respond when people ask "Where did you get it?" I usually just say something like "A store in San Francisco," rather than mention the thrift shop on Market Street. Friends who know me well don't even ask, because they know I could respond either Bloomingdale's or the Salvation Army, and at times it makes them want to go out and thrift shop, too. After all, everyone wants to get a bargain. I mostly mix my thrift-shopping finds with new so I can achieve "très chic" for "très cheap." A total look is still made up of parts, and by mixing the new with the original oldies, anyone or any place can look posh for pennies.

Identical trend patterns apply to furniture and household goods as well. Using a basic living room of an off-white sofa, upright piano, and oak wall unit, I can transform my living space into any look by changing the accessories. Adding three wrought-iron coffee tables ($20), big flowered tapestry pillows (fabric: $8, labor: my own), a revolving water-skier lamp ($2), and a stuffed club chair ($20), makes my room fifties kitsch. When I'm in the mood for art deco, I change the pillows, replace the coffee tables with a glass-top center table, and add some chromium knick knacks, my steel floor lamp ($3), and an art deco print in a carved frame ($7), and it doesn't cost much to make the changes. If I'm in the mood for the antique and homey look, I return again to my basic couch, piano, and wall unit and put in a pair of cherrywood torchères ($250 for the pair, but one of my all-time favorite purchases), carved wood picture frames with old photos in them, a coffee server (picked up on the street for free), and *voilà!* New look, new trend.

Buying to beat a trend requires the ability to recognize good design from an era. A Chanel suit from the sixties will look just as rich today as it did then. An oak sideboard of fine make will hold its elegance for fifty or one hundred years, so even if it is purchased secondhand, it still may have a few hands to go. Well-made and beautifully designed goods of any kind hold their beauty forever. Personally, I'd rather have gently used luxury than new things of lesser quality. Some things need to be bought and stored until their style returns; other things are classics that remain in style regardless of trends.

Quality clothing accessories can be easily stored and will transform an outfit the same way my furniture accessories changed my room. They are inexpensive to buy now and wear later. If I see unusual gloves, purses, jewelry, hats, or other accessories, I often pick them up for a song and stash them away until trends call them back. Five years ago I bought a sequined white sweater for $5, and this year I'd swear it was the same sweater on the cover of *Vogue* magazine. It takes a few dollars, a little foresight, and a bit of confidence to be ahead of the style.

When it comes to used appliances, I don't have a lot of luck. I once bought a great blender for $8 that cost me $60 to fix. Not a good buy. I bought a washer and dryer at a garage sale for $100 for both; the washer is terrific, but I still haven't found the right size replacement belt to make the dryer work. Sometimes it's worth the risk; sometimes you lose your shirt. You should try appliances before purchasing (I always do), but they are touchy and once moved don't always recover.

As a side note, I would like to point out that if you develop your foresight skills for trend buying, you can also sell your early-bought prizes when the style becomes hot. That $3 chromium floor lamp could fetch me a few hundred dollars at an antiques or consignment shop. The shop might sell it for $350, but I could still come out with a cool profit of almost $147 if I tell the shop my own price is $150. If you buy specifically for resale, you must be quite aware of what is in demand and what the market will bear. Of course, if I sell my lamp even for $25, I'll still make a profit because the buy price was so cheap. But there's a chance it may not sell and I may end up with it after all. I am convinced that half of all antiques dealers began their businesses with overflow of their personal purchases. Not a bad way to make money. In fact, there is currently a couple in New York City whose entire apartment is their store; all their furnish-

ings and accoutrements are for sale. Just pay a
visit and buy a piece from their home. How's that
for a new twist on "home shopping"?

More on Identifying Quality

"I'd rather have quality goods, used, than me-
diocre new."

—Jody Bamel

Even if you are not interested in spotting style
trends, it still behooves you to learn how to identify superior goods. No matter what the product,
there is always a top of the line and a bottom of
the barrel. Whether it be clothing, tools, housewares, jewelry, appliances, or whatever, there is
good quality and there is cheap imitation. As big
as a house or as small as an earring, the goal in
secondhand shopping is to buy good value at a low
price. In design, you will look for the trend that is
"now" or the classic that will always be in style:
When it comes to style, materials, and construction, you should always look for the best.

Design may be trendy or classic. Trendy may
mean kitsch or retro, as in the return of a popular
style from a bygone era. Trendy is not timeless;
it's hot and then it's not. The great thing about
buying trendy goods secondhand is that you can
be up-to-the-minute for a fraction of the price. You
can swap clothing, accessories, and household

goods in and out of fashion for a small price, while getting quality, uniqueness, and a fresh look every time. If you retain your big items, such as sofas and dresses, you can change their look by altering what is around them. For instance, take a simple navy dress and put on a sixties belt, with wild beads, and over-the-knee boots, and you have a fun, campy look. Using the same navy dress, go for pearls, pumps, and an evening bag, and you create a whole new style. Same dress, different appearance. The same applies to your furnishings: Surround your sofa with lava lamps and beanbag chairs, and you have one style. If you alter the accents to glass and brass, it takes on a more contemporary look.

Classic objects are timeless. Their look is neither in nor out. They have a feeling of elegance and continuity that never disappears. Classic design always looks good, no matter what the fashion trends dictate. A Federal-style armoire in cherry or maple will perpetually radiate beauty. Independent of what the world may call classic, in my definition "classic" means "design that I will never tire of"—simple and clean design that always pleases the wearer or the bearer. For me, Breuer chairs are classic. Russel Wright designs are classic. Anything produced by a well-known designer or manufacturer of any period is classic. Eames chairs, Chanel suits, Noguchi tables, Ferragamo pocketbooks, Stetson hats, and so on—all known in their day and beyond for having excellent design, materials, and construction—this is what classics are made of. Who knows? Someday maybe Air Jordans will be known as classics.

Good quality also consists of good materials and construction. If you don't know the designer name, you can look instead for the composition of the product and how it was put together. In clothing, you can read labels for contents and learn to feel with your fingers the difference between the natural and synthetic fibers. Natural fabrics like cotton, wool, and silk usually cost more when new and wear well over the years. This makes them likely candidates to be bought used and still be in good condition. Synthetics wear well also but usually don't look as fine used as naturals do. If you read labels and touch fabrics, you will eventually be able to identify the fabric whether there is a content label or not.

Natural fabrics look different from synthetics, and in time you will be able to pick them out on the racks with your eyes. I can spot a Gap T-shirt a mile away; its plush materials and sturdy construction stand out among the lesser goods. I look for good brand-name labels and inspect the materials and construction to use as future reference. Practicing and observing like this enables me to find quality in labels I may not recognize. Check for matching patterns (plaids and stripes should line up on either side of the seam), overcasting (the inside of the seams should be finished with thread or material to prevent unraveling), nice closures, buttonholes, and linings. Quality goods are put together well, have a full cut, and will look just as good tomorrow as they do today.

Although some of us are not interested in owning fur, I have heard of many incredible buys in this used-clothing category. Thrift shops and tag sales are the most likely places for the best buys, while the tag sellers seem to place a higher price tag on used fur coats and jackets than the thrift shops.

Older, out-of-date furs can be bought at reasonable prices. If they have been stored and cleaned and the hides are relatively supple, you may purchase them cheaply and bring them to a furrier for restyling. The price for alteration varies, depending on how much work needs to be done, (the inside of the seams should be finished with thread or material to prevent unraveling), so be careful not to create an entirely new garment that may cost more than it's worth when finished. A collar tuck here or a sleeve change there is usually worth the investment.

My friend Gloria bought a full-length mink about ten years old for $200 at a tag sale. She had the shoulders redone and the collar recut at a cost of $60. Not bad if mink is your cup of tea; the coat still cost less than a good wool new and looked like a million bucks. Gloria's sister-in-law tells me she snagged a mouton lamb jacket at the Salvation Army for a mere $15. She thought it was a fake fur when she found it tagged $25 with a rip in the inseam, so she asked the manager for a price reduction. The manager reduced the jacket to $15, and when she got it home and got ready to wash it, she noticed that the jacket was hide underneath the lining and not a fake at all. Her furrier repaired, cleaned, and glazed it for $40, and as luck would have it, the cuffed sleeves had just returned to fashion, so no major remodeling was necessary.

The best buy I've heard about was the purchase of a full ranch mink coat about a year old, hardly used, from Goodwill Industries for $175. The buyer took it off the rack, asked the price, and begged the manager to hold it for a half hour while she went to the cash machine. An unexpected find in April turned out to be the perfect winter cover-up appraised at $2,500!

When buying used fur, look for soft hides and full skins. Peek under the lining to see if the pieces are long and even instead of sewed together in sections. Check the nap of the fur from the top side; brush the fur backward and look for an underlayer of fur while inspecting the skin itself. If the fur and skin are both dark, they are probably dyed rather than natural. A yoked shoulder across the back is sometimes better made than just a plain sleeve-to-body attachment, and there should be no visible wear at the cuffs or pockets if the coat is fairly new. Split skins are cut in narrow slices (and leather strips connect them) while full skins have a wider spread between the leather. If you decide to search for a bargain in used fur, go to a few salons and ask questions. Touch and feel to learn about quality so you will have knowledge to shop with. The best bargains may be stumbled upon when you least expect them, so keep your eyes open and your cash card handy.

Looking for quality in construction materials applies to furniture as well. Look for stable legs, solid materials, and good finishes. The fabric can always be changed, so your biggest concern will be the piece's overall build. Well-constructed cabinets or dressers will have dovetail joints (interlocking wood instead of nails). A good sofa or chair is usually made with dowels and corner blocks which are wedges of wood in the niches for extra stability. They should also have webbing, a strong fabric woven in strips to provide support to the seats. Furniture built this way will most likely retain its shape without sagging for many years. Secondhand quality furniture will look wonderful with just a fabric change or refinishing. A facelift may be costly, however, so keep that in mind before making the investment in the piece.

Quality design, materials, and construction are things to look for in almost everything. Tools, ice buckets, dishes, and jewelry—all require the same inspection you give clothing and furniture. Look for excellent composition and proper function along with better materials. Good quality and design forty years ago will still be good quality and design today. Excellence endures.

How to Pick Your Prizes:
The Eyes Have It

"If you can't walk away from it—buy it. Life's too short to have small regrets."

—Dad Bamel

Okay, Dad. So I regret the Louis Vuitton steamer trunk I walked away from. It would have cost $150, and I couldn't figure out how to get it home or where to put it. That summer you showed me the *New York Times* ad for Louis Vuitton luggage, and a briefcase was $1,500. I only regret it a little. The lesson was worth the loss. And there have been plenty of things to make up for it.

From this incident I learned to trust my instinct on what was of value, and how sometimes you have to do anything you can to have what you want. I had a hunch from looking at the trunk that it was quality: leather and wood trim, all leather inside, and in perfect condition. If you're knowledgeable, you know what to buy. But you cannot know everything, so you have to trust your instincts and your eyes sometimes. Here are a few tips to help you decide what to buy.

1. Look for markings.
    Turn your item over and look for signatures

or logos of manufacturers. Read labels describing materials and see if they bear a name or mark you recognize. You can study these in books if you like. Tools, dishes, clothing, and furniture marks are printed in collectors' guides. Become familiar with them and the styles of design you are looking for, to help you spot the top-of-the-line goods. You don't need to memorize; *just recognize*. Repeat shopping and reading labels will educate you as well, just not as quickly. Remember, I studied depression glass markings so I could buy depression glass and trade it for my Russel Wright dishes.

2. Inspect item for degree of damage.

Look at furniture for rips, chips, scratches, and dents. Scrutinize clothing for snags, stains, and irreparable damage. In other words, don't buy it if it is beyond the amount of repair you will do or pay to have done, or if the damage will prevent you from using the item. Don't buy it if it is past its "expiration date."

3. Determine cleaning and repair costs.

Make an educated guess at how much time and money will need to be expended to bring the item to a condition to your liking. Weigh this against the price and decide whether or not it is worth the trouble. You can make this guess more educated by reading newspaper ads touting prices for reupholstery, cleaning, refinishing, etc. Again, I ask you to use your powers of observation for future reference.

4. Balance need and want.

Don't buy it if you really have no use for it, unless it is fairly cheap and there's a chance you may find a use for it later. I once passed up an old aluminum cooler that would have made a terrific toolbox, and it was only three bucks. I didn't think of the alternative use until it was too late. Which should also remind you to . . .

5. Use your imagination!!!!!!!!

Have foresight. Picture the item in your own home instead of among the litter. Try to picture it with a new coat of paint or a new fabric. Envision it as you would use it, which may not be what it was first designed for. The cosmetic traveling case I got for fifty cents made the perfect sewing box. Sometimes your use for an item may turn out to be better than its intended purpose.

6. Be aware of styles to come.

As mentioned before, new styles are often a return of the old. This is what makes it possible to buy quality goods from the original era before a more expensive version becomes available years later. Jewelry, art, clothing, and furniture styles also come around again, so look for it before it's hot and you'll be ahead of the style but behind in the price you will pay for it.

7. Remember friends and relatives when thrift shopping.
   Be open to possibilities of future gift-giving, especially if an item reminds you of someone. The item should be in gift-giving condition. Also, let friends and relatives know your taste so they can find great bargains for you, too. I love old luggage, so Marcy picked up a piece for me in her travels. Lots of people buy my collectibles when they find them. It is definitely the thought that counts.

8. Never buy just for the sake of buying.
   Don't buy something just to keep someone else from buying it. It's fine to walk away if you don't really want the item. There will be plenty of future bargains to spend your money on, so don't despair if there's nothing to buy.

9. Keep perspective on price.
   A dollar goes a long way when thrift shopping. It's annoying to pay $5 for a sweater when you just got an Eames chair for $4, but they may both be bargains. I've actually bought furniture that has cost less than a box of my favorite cereal, but it doesn't stop me from eating breakfast. Try to compare apples to apples.

10. Resell or donate your own castoffs.
    Even seasoned shoppers make a slipup here and there. Pass unwanted items on to thrift and consignment shops and see if you can recycle them.

Secondhand Sales on Sale

My brothers and sister-in-law taught me always to buy on sale. When the full price is marked down, it's time to make the purchase. Mostly I find secondhand buying to be a big enough bargain in the first place, but even secondhand items can get discounted. Many thrift and consignment shops have sales just like regular stores. I've seen dollar clothing sales, 40 or 50 percent off certain color tags—the Salvation Army does this routinely—and my all-time favorite: the bag or box sale. These are sales wherein you get a bag or a boxful for a preset price. The Salvation Army may charge $18 dollars or more per bag, but some are cheaper and may give you a plastic garbage bag to fill, and you can get five or six coats and an assortment of other things stuffed in before you reach the top. Churches and synagogues have bag and box sales as well, and I've stumbled upon a few bag sales at the end of the day at flea markets and garage sales when they are trying to get rid of the last of the wares. Many thrift stores have these sales at the end of the month or the close of a season, to clear out and make way for new goods. Ask the stores you frequent if they have bag sales and, if so, when they conduct them. Scout the store the week before for possible bag merchandise and then return early the day of the sale and collect the booty. On occasion, some of the things may be already gone, but never worry. There will always be another bag sale in the future.

Secondhand stores may also have markdown policies worth noting. I was in A Second Look in Phoenix, Arizona. They have a fine used furniture section along with an entire section of clothing and have an excellent policy I call "dating." Each item has a tag with a price and date on it. As you enter, a posted sign tells you after what date items will be 25% or 50% off. Items at least thirty days old are automatically reduced 25%, and items more than sixty days old are 50% off the original price. I had seen a great pair of newly donated Charles Jordan boots marked $62.00 and I wanted to wait the thirty days for them to be reduced. I asked my cousin Sandy (she lives in the area, and I live in New York) to go back to the store on the reduction date to get them for me, but they were already gone. I hadn't been willing to spend full price so I played the dating game and lost. I knew the risks and decided to take a chance. It's an old story, sometimes with a happy ending, sometimes not. I'm not too disappointed about it because I know there are plenty of bargains to be had.

Shopping and Shipping

A few friends and I are planning some shopping excursions this spring. One of them will be to two flea markets in Pennsylvania where a lot of dealers buy their goods. Another will be to the upstate New York auctions that my stepsister and her husband attend. The last will be to the new "garage sale" in New York City that includes groups of dealers and merchants housed in a multilevel parking-garage complex downtown. We will be prepared to bring back things from these planned trips. For Pennsylvania, we intend to drive out in a Bronco and rent a small truck or van to return with since we all want to buy furniture and would like to make sure we don't cramp our style by worrying about how to get it all home. We will reserve before we go to assure transportation for our finds. The architect, Glen, who told me about these markets said he went with a station wagon and filled it up the first day. He and his wife stayed overnight and, as luck would have it, ran into two of their neighbors who happened through at breakfast the next morning. They transferred all their stuff to the neighbors' station wagon and sent it home with them, giving Glen and his wife the opportunity to shop again and take home a second load!

On our upstate trek we will take a pickup and probably arrange for something small to hitch onto the back for the return ride. I have family there, so if we exceed our space, we can always leave some and come back again. But there's no need always to be so prepared. Don't let the question of shipping stop you from buying a bargain anywhere you might be. Anything can be shipped or delivered if you put your mind and money into finding a way.

In California I once bought a great pair of skates and went to the pack-and-ship; I sent them home for a mere $5. In Arizona I bought a set of luggage and had too many pieces to bring back on the plane, so I went to the post office and mailed it. I thought I needed a box, but the postal worker said since the luggage was rectangular and empty, all we had to do was tape it closed and put a label on it! The interesting thing is that it made it all the way across the country to my local New York post office, but my post office wouldn't deliver it because they said it wasn't regulation packing!

In Rochester, New York, I bought a beautiful bedroom set, and the store owner arranged to have it shipped to my home. It cost about $200, but even with the added cost of shipping it was a bargain.

You can look up local and long-distance movers yourself in any yellow pages and have things picked up and delivered by truck anywhere you want. At auctions you can often pay the auction house or anyone with a truck to get your purchases to a destination. Some of these locals will go pretty far within a three-hundred or four-hundred-mile radius, but if you want your goods insured, you will need the professionals. Some auctions and antique shows now have enterprising folks who rent their space to offer the service of shipping and delivery of customers' purchases. Quite convenient, even if the price is a little more than carting the items yourself.

Small tables, housewares, books, and other small items can be brought to shipping places like United Parcel Service if you are not too worried about them and don't want to carry them yourself. I have sent boxes of clothing, radios, dishes, and an assortment of other things home from my travels this way, just so I didn't have to lug them around with me. They only sometimes make it home before I do, but they almost always make it.

An acquaintance of mine shopped all over France for furnishings and arranged to have them shipped to his home on Long Island. Now, I'm not saying this was cheap; I'm just saying it is possible. He bought a fifteen-foot pewter bar from a place going out of business, along with some bar stools, tables, and an array of goods from different stores on his itinerary. He tells me that a moving company in England picked up each item one by one and packed and shipped them all to their offices in New York and then delivered them to his home, uncrated them, and set them all up. The moving company took care of the entire operation from soup to nuts. It may sound crazy, but if you've got the bread you can have your cake and eat it, too!

How to Bargain Down: Haggling the Price

There are a lot of people out there who are afraid to haggle a price. Granted, when you go into a department store, you usually don't ask the sales clerk for a discount or question the price. But at garage sales, tag sales, and flea markets, there is an open invitation to offer a price less than what is marked. This is half the fun of buying second-hand: the challenge of getting the best bargain possible. There is no reason to fear price dickering. The sellers aren't the enemy, merely folks trying to make a buck by selling their unwanted clutter. A fair price is difficult to assess in the beginning, but after a few sales even you will be able to see what asking prices are too high or too low.

While garage sale-ing in Maine with Gail, Erica, Ali, and Elaina, one of our purposes was to find an iron. At the first sale we saw one for $8. Way too high, considering you can buy a new one for about $15. At another sale we saw one for five, but I told Gail I thought this was still too much. Appliances and furniture should cost about one-fifth of the

price when new; clothing and small housewares about one-tenth of their original price. We finally found our iron for $1 at the last sale of the day. Not to mention paperbacks for ten cents apiece, T-shirts for fifty cents, and a few pairs of jeans for two dollars each. Mostly the price is dependent upon what you or someone else will be willing to pay.

At an earlier sale the same day, Gail spotted some educational Fisher-Price tapes. The set was in excellent condition, along with its original box and instructions. The seller was a grandmother and had only let the children listen to the tapes while supervised, so they were used but not abused. The asking price was $30, and Gail knew they sold for about sixty when new. She was reluctant to haggle so she asked me to. The first question I asked Gail was "What is the highest price you will pay for them?" She responded with "Fifteen dollars." I approached the seller again and asked her humbly if she would she take ten. She rejected the offer but countered at twenty dollars. I came back at fifteen, and although she wouldn't accept fifteen, she said she would take eighteen. Gail decided it was worth the extra three dollars, so she made the purchase and came home with a fine gift for the next Christmas.

There are a few guidelines to help you do the bargain-down. The main rule is to decide the maximum price you are willing to pay. This may be flexible at the end, but it gives you a set point to work from. If you know your price is low, be humble and gentle when making the offer, so as not to insult the seller. However low your offer, don't be dissuaded from making it. Just remember that the item was once a treasure of the owner, and he or she has some knowledge of its worth, so don't be brash.

When you make your offer, make it for less than your maximum price. There's a chance you may get it on the first offer, but not usually, which is why you need to leave a little room for the counter offer. The most the person can say is no, but more often than not he or she will come back with another price. For example, you've seen a chair you want that is tagged $50. You would like to buy it for twenty-five. Offer the seller twenty, and he or she may counter at thirty. Next, go up to your preset twenty-five and see if you can't walk away with it. It doesn't work all the time, but it's worth a shot. If there is no counter offer, and you want the item badly enough, you may have to change your preset limit or walk away. I would like to note that if the seller comes back at you with a price much lower than what is marked, this is a signal that you may have greater bargaining power than you think. Always try to read the subliminal signs when bargaining.

Sometimes the seller will approach you while you are inspecting an item, and *tell* you that the price is negotiable! A pretty clear signal, even for the squeamish haggler. At this point consider offering less than you thought. Perhaps sales aren't going well that day and the owner is anxious to clear out the goods at any price. There are other signals that are just as important but not as easy to see.

At flea markets and fairs, always take notice of the other shoppers. Are they carrying bags of purchases? If not, the prices may be marked too high, the goods may not be so great, the bartering power may be limited, or this may simply be a slow sale day. If the latter is the case, take advantage of your ability to haggle, and you may go home a winner.

An important thing to remember when price dickering is to *be nice*. The owner wants to sell the item, and if it has sentimental value, she or he will want to sell it to someone who is appreciative. There may be a history attached to the article, and I for one always encourage the seller to tell it. I remember buying a nightstick a while back from a nice woman's barn sale. She was happy to tell me how her Uncle Bob had carried it on his beat in Brooklyn in the 1930s. This helped me date it and give it its place of origin. Her uncle sounded

like a terrific guy, and when I told her I wanted
the stick as a gift for someone who would be using
it for a similar purpose, as well as how much the
gift would be appreciated, she sold it to me for a
few dollars without even dickering over the price.
The seller was happy to let it go to someone who
would really want it and who understood her sen-
timents. Money isn't always everything when it
comes to good memories. The recipient of the
nightstick was equally interested in its story,
which gave meaning to a simple piece of wood.

At private sales you will have more bartering
power at the end of the day. If the sale is over at
4 P.M.. and it is 3:30, be bold. A small profit is better than no profit in most people's eyes. If it is
early in the day, sellers may hold out for a better
price, but you can return later to see if you can
acquire items cheap. Although there is little bartering power at thrift shops, it is important to get
to know the owners or volunteers. Regular customers can get preferential treatment. If you frequent the same shop and you are always nice, you
will be remembered and you will have the ability
to ask for better prices even if it is not the norm.
You must ask nicely if they will reduce the price
for you, and sometimes they will. Even if the answer is no, there is no harm done.

When I was in college, near my school there was
a store called the Price Is Right. I often went there
to buy small things and ogle the things I couldn't
have. My girlfriend and I had seen a crocheted

bedspread for $30, which was a lot at the time. My friend and I both wanted it badly, but neither of us could afford it. I returned to the store periodically, just to browse and talk to the owner, who had many tales to tell. At close of semester I stopped in on my way home and asked her about the bedspread I so admired. I told her I had $15 to spare above my travel expenses, and she sold me the bedcover. I look back now and remember the lesson: Nice pays off. Yes, my girlfriend is still mad at me for getting the bedspread so cheap, but she has since made her own great finds, and we have both met some interesting people in our shopping travels.

I don't know if I should mention the bedroom set I saw at the Price is Right. It is still a sore spot; one of those regretted missed opportunities. There was an art deco bedroom set with inlaid woods for sale. It had two nightstands, one dresser with mirror, and one tall chest. The asking price was $500, which was the cost of an entire semester of classes back then. I thought about begging to borrow the money, but I kept asking myself, How am I going to get it home? and Where am I going to put it? Both sensible questions. I thought about it no further until two years later, when my friend Bob and I were at a swanky antiques store called Thirties Forties and there was the bedroom set with one less dresser. The price? Thirteen thousand dollars! I went white and almost fainted. These things happen when you shop the thrift. There

will be a few losses, but you *may* make up for them
with the wins. Anyway, you can always applaud
yourself for recognizing the value, and attempting
to bargain down to what you can afford. You see,
that is my main regret in this case. I never even
tried to buy the set, when all along I had nothing
to lose by making an offer. The lesson to be learned
is: Make all reasonable offers. Try to leave a deposit or arrange to pay in parts if you cannot pay
the full price all at once. Some thrift stores even
accept credit cards now, so you can pay on "time"
if you want it enough. There is no risk involved,
only something to gain.

For Your Information

The number of possible places to do second-hand shopping increases constantly. Finding these places sometimes calls for research, but usually you need only to pay attention in your daily activities to discover them. I have previously mentioned the yellow pages, local shopping newspapers, and the Classified sections of the major news publications as excellent and simple sources for shops and sales. There are a variety of other ways to locate places and information not to be overlooked.

In many areas there are home-shopping channels on television where people advertise goods and sales. You can tune in and shop from your couch without even leaving your living room. Friends and relatives always keep me informed about the good flea markets, shows, and sales they have attended, so don't forget to swap information with the people you know.

In my day job I work with a lot of decorators and architects, and many of them are dedicated antiques and bargain shoppers who have searched for and found great sources of quality merchandise at good prices. My sisters and cousins, my brothers and friends, my father, my friends' parents, and lots of people who know me have found me countless sources for the Russel Wright I collect, because they now know what to look for. In return I buy them a bargain of their own liking. There are times when we strike out, but most of the time we succeed in finding things for one another that we can use. So remember to ask and tell.

When you travel, stop at tourist information centers or rest stops and look for brochures and flyers to tell you where to find flea markets, auctions, swap meets, and whatever other large sales and shows take place in the area. I pick them up whether or not I'll be going immediately, because you never know about the future. I keep a file in my cabinet at home market "Sales," where I stuff all my tidbits for future reference. My friend Glen keeps his filed by state, but I don't travel as much as he does and I'm not quite that organized, so one folder works for me. Be sure to pick up flyers and brochures from the resale shops, markets, and shows you have already found. You may find notices of special sales and bag days, postings from consignments shops of goods they accept, and even mailing lists or newsletters for future events.

The library is my favorite source for just about

everything. There are phone books from all over the country, so you can look things up prior to travel. They have volumes on specific collectibles and markings, and pricing books such as the Kovels' guides to antiques and collectibles. I often peruse furniture and collectible books just to become familiar with what I might see on a spree. On my last library sojurn, I found a wonderful book called *Official Directory to U.S. Flea Markets,* edited by Kitty Werner, which has detailed descriptions of flea markets, including their locations, merchandise, and dates. Another book of interest is *The Tightwad Gazette,* by Amy Dacyczyn, which has many hints on thrift as a general lifestyle. At the library you will also find antiques magazines and, of course, newspapers to look through for more places to hunt for treasures. If you are in search of something specific and there is a book on the subject, it may pay to purchase it so you can take it with you. I wouldn't recommend bringing it into a garage or tag sale, because you don't want the sellers to know the value of your collectible—that would invariably jack up the price—but you can leave the book in your car for reference.

During the past few years I have noticed articles in major newspapers and magazines about auctions, decorating on a budget, and flea-market finds. At times I'll be reading a seemingly unrelated item about some fancy residence, and there will be a reference to a piece of furniture or an accessory acquired at a garage sale. It pays to read widely just to pick up a hint or two. It is typical of me to cut articles out and put them in my sales file in case I need to look at them later, but there's no need to be as obsessive as I am. Just reading the articles will suffice. Keep your eyes and ears open and you will always learn something new—maybe a shopping strategy or a new show or place to browse.

There is currently a group called the National Association of Resale & Thrift Shops, founded by Trudy Miller, that you can write to for a list of shop members. This is not a consumer group—it is for merchants, so please don't call them—but you can get their list of resale shop members by sending your request and a self-addressed, stamped envelope with $3 (current price) to NARTS, 20331 Mack Avenue, Grosse Pointe Woods, MI 48236. They also publish a consumer newsletter of general info to increase shopping skills, called *Resale Details,* which comes out four times a year and has a subscription price of $10. It is not a large newsletter, but it has interesting tips and updates to help secondhand shoppers.

There are no exact statistics, complete lists, or single sources for secondhand sales, which is why I am giving you all the tips I can on how to compile your own. Secondhand shopping has increased tremendously in the past few years, although some of us have been addicted for years. Buying resale and donating to thrift and consignment shops give us the opportunity to recycle and share our prized possessions and our unwanted odds and ends.

Fix-Up Hints

I don't have many of my own fix-up hints; I learned a lot from *Mary Ellen's Helpful Hints* and picked up a few others along the way. The few that I do know come in very handy, however, so I will pass them along.

Clothing

Many very good wool sweaters pill and fuzz. Those little wool balls are easy to remove with a basic double-edged razor. Just stretch the sweater taut a section at a time, and lightly run your razor over it. The whole process usually takes about ten to fifteen minutes for an entire sweater, but it can save a few garments from extinction. If a sweater is in good condition except for pilling, you can take a chance on buying it and de-fuzz it when you get home. Be careful that the sweater is not too far gone to be saved; stains and shrinkage are almost uncorrectable when it comes to wool.

Cottons have a better chance for stain removal. White cotton often has yellow discoloration caused by dry-cleaning chemicals. I got this recipe for stain removal from my friend Monika, but be sure to do this outdoors with rubber gloves. The odor is quite potent, and I'm sure the solution is, too, so avoid breathing the fumes. Mix one cup of Clorox 2 with one cup of Ajax floor cleaner (the one in the yellow bottle) in a big bucket and add water. Submerge the garment overnight, rinse in the morning, and eventually rewash. I have done this on light-colored cottons even with prints, but it can't be done to red or black. This stain remover won't work on everything, but it is a good last resort when the only other choice is to toss the item out.

The last quick fix I know is alteration. A good seamstress or tailor can alter a piece of clothing to your requirements, but it may be a bit costly to have done. I buy suits made of great material, and at a size or two too big, because they are worth tailoring at $35 a piece, especially if the suit price is five, ten, or fifteen dollars.

Furniture

Furniture fixes are not often fast or easy. A good polish with Old English or another good polish will cover and fill small scratches. A good cleaning with Formby's or other wood cleaner can reveal a beautiful wood finish under layers of wax. My brother Jerry bought a Heywood-Wakefield dining table with a discolored leaf. The refinisher recommended a serious cleaning before stripping, and lo and behold, the whole table was one color underneath. Cleaning alone does not always bring back luster, however, and refinishing can be expensive or time-consuming. If you decide to do it yourself, be honest. If the piece of furniture will hang around your garage waiting years to be sanded and stained, it may not be worth buying. I know I won't ever actually do this myself so I restrict myself to purchasing only what it pays to get reupholstered or refinished. I currently own three unmatched chairs that will eventually get coordinating fabrics on them when I get a couch and am ready to choose fabric. The cost of this can be close to what a brand-new chair would go for, but the chairs are exactly the style I wanted, and their prices were $20, $8, and free. I'll get the custom look I want and the quality I desire, at a reasonable price.

Dishes and Glassware

Glassware at thrift shops and garage sales is often crusty with dirt. A good dishwashing or light scrubbing with steel wool may reveal a sparkle below the surface. Inspect glass and dishes closely for scratches. If most of the crust is dirt, a good wash can leave your glass spotless. I also find it helpful to soak vases and glasses with hard-to-reach places by filling them with warm water and dropping denture-cleaning tablets into them. This will sometimes release the grime without much effort. Bleach tile cleaners work well on glazed ceramics but may fade out decals or painted surface designs. My theory is this: If the item is cheap enough, I'll take a shot at it. Some are winners and some are losers, but it's a fun surprise when you uncover the beauty below the surface.

Shopping Tools

Supplies Checklist

1. A vehicle that packs a lot.
2. Cash in small denominations (change, singles, fives, and tens).
3. Map and street atlas.
4. Moist towelettes to clean your hands after touching all kinds of items of unknown origin.
5. Tape measure or equal. (I know my finger spread is eight inches, and my sneakers are ten inches, so I use them in a pinch.)
6. Magnet to test metals. Magnets stick to iron and cheap base metals, but won't stick to brass, copper, silver, or bronze.
7. Magnifing glass to read small or hard-to-see identifying marks on just about anything.
8. Fabric swatches, paint chips, pieces of tile or moldings, or anything else you need to do shopping "match-ups" for existing rooms or clothing.
9. A partner and copilot (optional).
10. A smile (not optional).

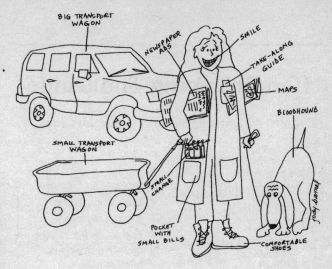

Buying Guide

1. Scan and seek before closer examination.
2. Pick up possible purchases.
3. Look for identifying marks.
4. Inspect goods for degree of damage.
5. Determine need and want.
6. Use your imagination.
7. Be aware of trends.
8. Keep perspective on price.
9. Decide maximum price before haggling.
10. Don't buy for the sake of buying.
11. Remember friends and relatives for gifts.

Handy Take-Along Guide

(Cut out, fold, and carry with you at all times.)

BUYING GUIDE

1. Scan and seek before closer examination.
2. Pick up possible purchases.
3. Look for identifying marks.
4. Inspect goods for degree of damage.
5. Determine need and want.
6. Use your imagination.
7. Be aware of trends.
8. Keep perspective on price.
9. Decide maximum price before haggling.
10. Don't buy for the sake of buying.
11. Remember friends and relatives for gifts.

Fold here

SUPPLIES CHECKLIST

1. A vehicle that packs a lot.
2. Cash in small denominations.
3. Map and street atlas.
4. Moist towelettes to clean your hands after touching all kinds of items of unknown origin.
5. Tape measure or equal. (I know my finger spread is eight inches and my sneakers are ten inches, so I use them in a pinch.)
6. Magnet to test metals. Magnets stick to iron and cheap base metals, but won't stick to brass, copper, silver, or bronze.
7. Magnifying glass to read small or hard-to-see identifying marks on just about anything.
8. Fabric swatches, paint chips, pieces of tile or moldings, or anything else you need to do shopping "match-ups" for existing rooms or clothing.
9. A partner and copilot (optional).
10. A smile (not optional).

When to Thrift Shop

IT'S TIME FOR A POP POP QUIZ!

Jody Bamel

Quiz Question:

When do you stop thrift shopping?

    a. When you're out of time
    b. When you're out of money
    c. When your car is full
    d. Never
    e. All of the above

Answer: e

Last Notes

I have written this book with the intention of adding knowledge and enjoyment to the art of secondhand shopping. To the best of my knowledge, the stories are genuine and factual. I have relied on my experience and research, along with the suggestions of others, to reveal the secrets of the most successful shoppers—including myself, if I may be so bold! The thrift-shopping experience is best understood by those who have done it and by those who are now ready to try it; it is certainly not the same as a trip to the mall. The advice in this book should serve as a guide and should not be viewed as a guarantee of price, quality, or method.

When you shop department stores, you will see forty of the same thing in a variety of colors. When you thrift shop, you will be seeking the unique, unusual, and cheap; collectibles, one-of-a-kind treasures, and assortments of everything will abound. Don't be afraid to dig. A boxful of junk may have a prize at the bottom that hasn't been uncovered yet.

Have fun, use your imagination, and enjoy your new hobby. Cut out the Handy Take-Along Guide to carry in your wallet at all times. Keep your supplies with you, in your vehicle, purse, knapsack or whatever. You never know when you might come across a hot sale, and you won't want to pass up the opportunity to score a bargain. Often it is the unexpected stop that yields the most success. Welcome to the world of secondhand shopping and don't forget: Save some for me!

Dedication

This book is dedicated to all the friends, relatives, and acquaintances who have been with me through all my years of thrift shopping, to all the people in my life who are afraid to ask, "Where did you get it?" and to all my loved ones who eternally give their support. I have included this last so that if you don't want to you won't feel guilty about not reading all the names. If your name is not on the list, I thank you, too, just for reading this guide. Happy shopping to everyone, and remember: The dollars may be shrinking, but the avenues to spend them are always wide open!

Thanks,
Sol*Selma*Isadore*Fannie*Bubbie*Jerry*Art*
Fran*Steven*Jonathan*Carolyn*Jimmy*Eva*
Len*Bea*Sol*Loretta*Sandy*Tony*Andrea*
Don*Linda*Eddie*Barry*Robert*Kathy*Kelly*
Ray*Kim*Bill*Kurt*Mark*Mary*Penny*Mike*
Viki*Mike*Karen*Joe*Bet*Duke*Drew*Bonnie
*Robyn*Markie*Wayne*Debbie*Marcy*Matt*
Linda*Andy*Lois*Roxanne*Rob*Cheryl*Walter
*Rob*Donna*Dennis*Wayne*Ron*John*Rosemary*Mark*Lillian*Eileen*Chris*Bob*Shirley*

Susan * Chet * Joyce * Milton * Chip * Marie * Sue *
Nancy * Bobee G. * Carol * Morty * Shirley * Debo-
rah * Mark * Vinny * Bob * Jon * Monika * Elise * Me-
gan * Bryan * Jordan * Charles * Ingrid * Mr. Blouin
* Mr. Fox * Marion * Smitty * Jay * Carol * Chris *
Charlies * Monica * Peggy * Eric * John * Gail * Vicky
* Kenny * Steven * Jeff * Maria * Vivian * Larry * Gary
* Howard * Sparky * Kahlua * Nancy * Frank * Mindy
* Sheldon * Rena * Vincent * Bill * June * Cary * Neil *
Ed * Neil * Barbara * Cousin Adolph * Molly * Bob *
Russell * Olive * Professor Jackson * Kiersten *
Courtney * Matt * Zach * Erica * Ryan * Dennis * Ed *
Blair * Sarah * Zach * Elyse * Jason * Brittany * Glen *
The Dolinkys * Maureen * Laurie * Bob * Tony C. *
Emily * Carey * Sam * Jordan * Chris * Ellen * Kenny
* Erica * Elaina Jo * Angie * Ali * Ike * Suzanne *
Harvey * Betty * Greg * Debbie * Artie * Brendan *
Lindsay * Bill * Toni * Ram * Carl * Betty * Don * Jim *
Ron * Steven * Jamie * Sue.

The last thanks but the most important is to my
parents, because no one deserves it more than they
do.

Bibliography

Kovels' Antiques & Collectibles Price List
Ralph & Terry Kovel
New York: Crown Publishers

The Tightwad Gazette
Amy Dacyczyn
New York: Villard Books
1992

Official Directory to U.S. Flea Markets
Edited by Kitty Werner
New York: House of Collectibles/Ballantine
1994

Mary Ellen's Best of Helpful Hints
Pearl Higginbotham and Mary Ellen Pinkham
New: Warner Books/B. Lansky Books
1979